Farm Life
Coloring Book

An Adult Coloring Book Featuring Charming
Country Farm Scenes and Beautiful Farm Animals
for Stress Relief and Relaxation

an Imprint of **The Fruitful Mind Publishing LTD.**

www.coloringbookcafe.com

Have questions? Let us know.

support@coloringbookcafe.com

 facebook.com/coloringbookcafe    @coloringbookcafe

This Book
Belongs To:

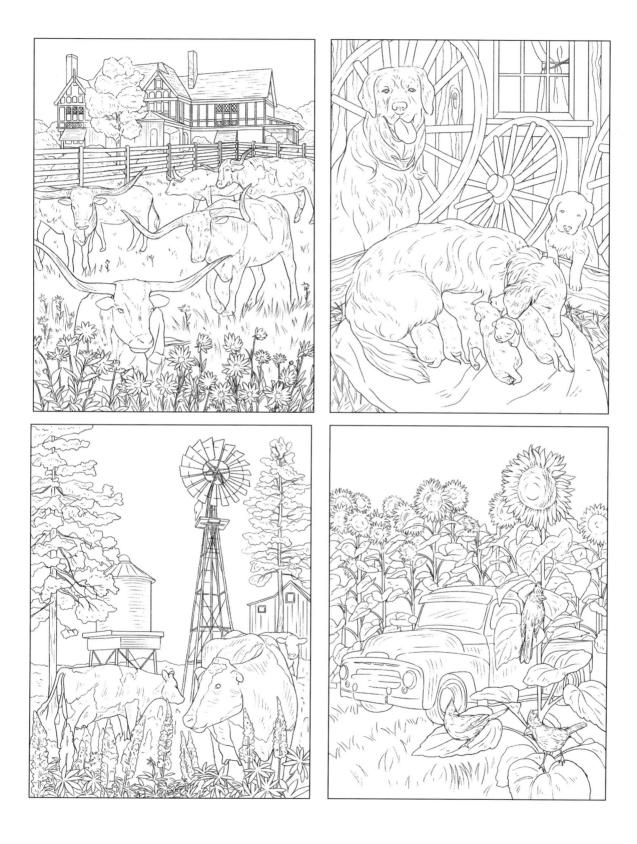

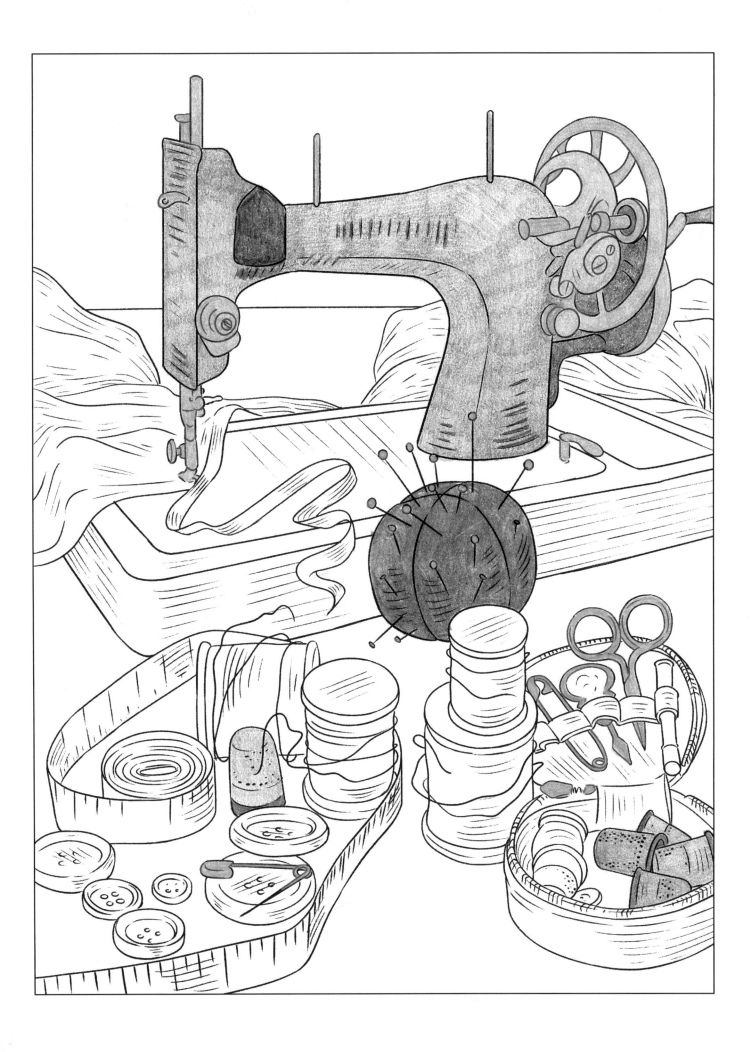

Made in United States
Orlando, FL
07 May 2022

17641125R00046